The Ultimate Guide To Successful Parenting: Proven Strategies For Raising Happy And Responsible Kids

Negoita Manuela

Published by Negoita Manuela, 2024.

THE ULTIMATE GUIDE TO SUCCESSFUL PARENTING: PROVEN STRATEGIES FOR RAISING HAPPY AND RESPONSIBLE KIDS

First edition. March 31, 2024.

Copyright © 2024 Negoita Manuela.

ISBN: 979-8224699780

Written by Negoita Manuela.

Table of Contents

Chapter 1: Introduction

- The importance of parenting in a child's development

Parenting plays a crucial role in a child's development, as it influences various aspects of their physical, emotional, social, and cognitive growth. The way parents interact with their children, set boundaries, provide support, and nurture their well-being can have a lasting impact on their overall development. Research has consistently shown that positive parenting practices lead to better outcomes for children, while negative or inconsistent parenting can lead to emotional and behavioral issues. Therefore, understanding the importance of parenting and its impact on child development is essential for parents, caregivers, educators, and policymakers.

One of the key aspects of parenting that can greatly influence a child's development is the quality of the parent-child relationship. A warm, supportive, and secure attachment between a child and their parent can foster a sense of trust, security, and emotional well-being. Children who have secure attachments with their parents are more likely to develop healthy relationships, have higher self-esteem, and better regulate their emotions. On the other hand, children who experience neglect, abuse, or inconsistent care from their parents may struggle with self-esteem issues, trust, and emotional regulation. Therefore, building a strong and positive parent-child relationship is essential for promoting healthy development in children.

In addition to the emotional aspects of parenting, the way parents set boundaries, provide discipline, and teach values to their children also plays a critical role in their development. Effective discipline strategies that are fair, consistent, and age-appropriate can help children learn self-control, responsibility, and respect for others. Parents who use positive reinforcement, clear expectations, and appropriate consequences are more likely to raise children who are well-behaved, self-disciplined, and able to navigate social situations effectively. On the other hand, parents who use harsh or inconsistent discipline strategies may inadvertently promote negative behaviors, aggression, and defiance in their children. Therefore, it is important for parents to develop positive discipline techniques that promote healthy behavior and positive development in their children.

Furthermore, the way parents support their children's learning, exploration, and interests can also have a profound impact on their cognitive development. Parents who are actively involved in their children's education, provide stimulating activities, and encourage curiosity and learning are more likely to raise children who are motivated, academically successful, and curious about the world around them. In contrast, parents who are disengaged, uninvolved, or critical of their children's interests may hinder their cognitive development and academic success. Therefore, it is important for parents to be actively engaged in their children's learning, provide opportunities for exploration and growth, and support their intellectual development in a positive and encouraging manner. The quality of the parent-child relationship, the way parents set boundaries and provide discipline, and the level of support parents offer for their children's learning and interests all contribute to the overall well-being and development of the child. Therefore, understanding the importance of parenting and its impact on child development is essential for parents, caregivers, educators, and policymakers. By promoting positive parenting practices, building strong parent-child relationships, setting clear boundaries, and supporting children's learning and growth, we can help ensure that every child has the opportunity to thrive and reach their full potential.

- Setting the foundation for successful parenting

Parenting is a complex and challenging task that requires careful consideration and planning. Setting the foundation for successful parenting is crucial in ensuring a healthy and thriving relationship between parents and children. By establishing strong communication, setting clear boundaries, and providing consistent support, parents can create a safe and nurturing environment for their children to grow and develop.

One of the most important aspects of successful parenting is communication. Effective communication between parents and children is essential for building trust, understanding, and connection. Parents should strive to create an open and supportive environment where their children feel comfortable expressing their thoughts, feelings, and concerns. By actively listening to their children and showing empathy and understanding, parents can strengthen their bond and nurture a positive relationship.

Setting clear boundaries is another key element in successful parenting. Boundaries help children understand expectations, rules, and limits, which are essential for their growth and development. Parents should establish rules and consequences that are fair, reasonable, and consistent. By enforcing boundaries in a calm and respectful manner, parents can teach their children important life skills, such as responsibility, self-discipline, and respect for others.

Consistent support is also critical in setting the foundation for successful parenting. Parents should be a source of love, encouragement, and guidance for their children, providing them with the emotional and practical support they need to navigate the challenges of growing up. By being present, involved, and available, parents can help their children build resilience, confidence, and self-esteem.

In addition to communication, boundaries, and support, there are several other factors that contribute to successful parenting. These include positive discipline, role modeling, and self-care. Positive discipline involves using gentle, respectful, and effective strategies to guide children's behavior and teach them valuable lessons. By modeling positive behaviors, values, and attitudes, parents can inspire and motivate their children to follow their lead. Self-care is also important for parents to prioritize their well-being and mental health, which in turn, enables them to be the best possible parents for their children. By focusing on building strong communication, setting clear boundaries, providing consistent support, practicing positive discipline, modeling positive behavior, and prioritizing self-care, parents can create a nurturing and loving environment for their children to thrive. Successful parenting is a journey that requires ongoing effort, learning, and growth, but ultimately, the rewards of raising happy, healthy, and resilient children are priceless.

Chapter 2: Understanding Your Child's Behavior

- Recognizing different behavior patterns in children

Children exhibit a wide range of behaviors, and it is important for parents, educators, and caregivers to be able to recognize and understand these behavior patterns. By being aware of the different behaviors that children may display, adults can better support and guide children in their development. There are several key behavior patterns that are commonly seen in children, including aggressive behavior, withdrawn behavior, and attention-seeking behavior. By recognizing and understanding these patterns, adults can provide appropriate interventions and support to help children navigate their emotions and behaviors in a healthy way.

One common behavior pattern that children may exhibit is aggressive behavior. This can manifest in a variety of ways, including physical aggression (such as hitting or biting), verbal aggression (such as yelling or name-calling), or relational aggression (such as spreading rumors or excluding others). Aggressive behavior in children can be a response to a variety of underlying issues, such as frustration, lack of emotional regulation skills, or exposure to violence or conflict in their environment. It is important for adults to recognize and address aggressive behavior in children, as it can have negative consequences for both the child and those around them.

Another behavior pattern that children may exhibit is withdrawn behavior. This can include behaviors such as isolating themselves, avoiding social interactions, or refusing to participate in activities. Withdrawn behavior in children may be a sign of underlying issues such as anxiety, depression, or low self-esteem. It is important for adults to recognize and address withdrawn behavior in children, as it can impact their social and emotional development. By providing support and encouragement, adults can help children overcome their withdrawn behavior and engage more fully in their environment.

Attention-seeking behavior is another common behavior pattern that children may display. This can include behaviors such as seeking constant validation or approval, being overly dramatic or showy, or engaging in disruptive behaviors to gain attention. Attention-seeking behavior in children may be a sign of underlying issues such as low self-esteem, unmet emotional needs, or a lack of positive reinforcement in their environment. It is important for adults to recognize and address attention-seeking behavior in children, as it can impact their relationships with others and their ability to regulate their emotions. By providing positive attention and encouragement for more positive behaviors, adults can help children develop healthier ways of seeking attention.

In addition to these common behavior patterns, children may also exhibit a variety of other behaviors that can be indicative of underlying issues or challenges. For example, children who are struggling with learning disabilities or developmental delays may exhibit behaviors such as difficulty focusing, impulsivity, or frustration with tasks. Children who have experienced trauma or adverse experiences may exhibit behaviors such as aggression, withdrawal, or emotional dysregulation. By recognizing and understanding these behaviors, adults can provide appropriate interventions and support to help children navigate their challenges and develop healthy coping mechanisms. By being aware of the various behaviors that children may exhibit, adults can better understand the underlying issues and challenges that children may be facing. This knowledge can inform interventions and strategies to help children develop healthy coping mechanisms, regulate their emotions, and navigate their social interactions in a positive way. By fostering a supportive and understanding environment, adults can help children thrive and reach their full potential.

- Identifying potential underlying causes of behavior issues

Behavior issues can be complex and multifaceted, stemming from a variety of underlying causes. It is important to approach behavior issues with a holistic perspective, considering not only the observable behaviors themselves but also the potential factors that may be driving them. By identifying and addressing these underlying causes, we can effectively support individuals in managing their behavior and improving their overall well-being.

One potential underlying cause of behavior issues is social and emotional factors. Individuals may exhibit challenging behaviors as a way of expressing their emotions or seeking attention. For example, a child who is struggling with feelings of insecurity or low self-esteem may act out in disruptive ways in an attempt to gain validation or control. Additionally, social factors such as peer pressure or conflicts within relationships can also contribute to behavior issues. By addressing these social and emotional needs through supportive interventions and strategies, we can help individuals develop more positive coping mechanisms and healthier ways of expressing themselves.

Another common underlying cause of behavior issues is environmental factors. The environment in which an individual lives and learns can have a significant impact on their behavior. For example, a chaotic or unstable home environment may contribute to feelings of stress or anxiety, leading to disruptive behaviors. Additionally, factors such as exposure to violence, substance abuse, or poverty can also have a negative impact on behavior. By creating a supportive and structured environment that promotes safety, security, and positive relationships, we can help individuals feel more stable and secure, reducing the likelihood of behavior issues.

Cognitive and developmental factors can also play a role in behavior issues. Individuals who have cognitive or developmental challenges may struggle to effectively regulate their emotions or behavior. For example, a child with ADHD may have difficulty focusing or controlling their impulses, leading to impulsive or hyperactive behaviors. Additionally, individuals with autism spectrum disorders may have difficulty with social communication and interactions, which can manifest in challenging behaviors. By understanding and addressing these cognitive and developmental challenges through appropriate accommodations and supports, we can help individuals manage their behavior more effectively and thrive in their environments.

Trauma and adverse experiences are another potential underlying cause of behavior issues. Individuals who have experienced trauma, abuse, or neglect may exhibit challenging behaviors as a way of coping with their past experiences. For example, a child who has been exposed to violence or abuse may display aggressive or antisocial behaviors as a means of self-protection. Additionally, individuals who have experienced loss or separation may struggle with feelings of grief or abandonment, leading to emotional dysregulation and acting out behaviors. By providing trauma-informed care and support, we can help individuals process their past experiences and develop healthier coping mechanisms for managing their behavior.

In closing, biological factors such as genetics and neurodiversity can also contribute to behavior issues. Some individuals may be genetically predisposed to certain behavioral patterns or mental health conditions, such as anxiety or depression. Additionally, individuals with neurodevelopmental disorders such as autism or ADHD may have unique brain functioning that influences their behavior. By understanding and addressing these biological factors through appropriate interventions and supports, we can help individuals manage their behavior and thrive in their environments. By taking a holistic approach to identifying and addressing these underlying causes, we can effectively support individuals in managing their behavior and improving their overall well-being. By working collaboratively with individuals, families, and professionals from various disciplines, we can develop comprehensive interventions and strategies that promote positive behavior and well-being for all individuals.

Chapter 3: Effective Communication with Your Child

- Building strong communication skills with your child

Building strong communication skills with your child is essential for fostering a healthy and positive relationship. Effective communication is the key to understanding your child's thoughts, feelings, and needs, and it also helps to build trust and create a strong bond between parent and child. By developing strong communication skills, parents can help their children navigate through challenges, express themselves confidently, and develop important social skills that will serve them well in all aspects of their lives.

One of the most important aspects of building strong communication skills with your child is active listening. Active listening involves giving your full attention to your child when they are speaking, acknowledging their feelings, and responding in a way that shows understanding and empathy. By actively listening to your child, you are showing them that their thoughts and feelings are important to you, which helps to strengthen your bond and build trust. It is important to remember that communication is a two-way street, and listening is just as important as speaking in a successful communication exchange.

In addition to active listening, it is important to create an open and supportive environment for communication with your child. This means creating a safe space where your child feels comfortable expressing themselves without fear of judgment or criticism. Encourage open and honest communication by being approachable, non-judgmental, and supportive. Let your child know that they can come to you with any concerns or problems, and that you are there to listen and help. By creating a supportive environment for communication, you are helping to build your child's confidence and encouraging them to open up and share their thoughts and feelings with you.

Another important aspect of building strong communication skills with your child is asking open-ended questions. Open-ended questions are questions that cannot be answered with a simple "yes" or "no," and encourage your child to think critically and express themselves in more detail. By asking open-ended questions, you are encouraging your child to expand on their thoughts, feelings, and experiences, and helping them to develop their communication skills. Open-ended questions can also help you to better understand your child's perspective and gain insight into their thoughts and feelings.

In addition to active listening, creating a supportive environment, and asking open-ended questions, it is also important to be patient and respectful when communicating with your child. Remember that communication is a process, and it may take time for your child to feel comfortable opening up and expressing themselves. Be patient and give your child the space and time they need to process their thoughts and emotions. Respect your child's feelings and opinions, even if they differ from your own, and show them that you value their perspective. By being patient and respectful, you are building a strong foundation for communication and fostering a positive and healthy relationship with your child. By actively listening, creating a supportive environment, asking open-ended questions, and being patient and respectful, parents can help their children develop important communication skills that will serve them well in all aspects of their lives. Effective communication not only strengthens the bond between parent and child, but also helps children navigate through challenges, express themselves confidently, and develop important social skills. By investing time and effort into building strong communication skills with your child, you are setting the stage for a strong and supportive relationship that will last a lifetime.

- Navigating difficult conversations with your child

Having difficult conversations with your child can be a challenging and intimidating experience for many parents. Whether the topic is related to sensitive issues such as sexuality, substance abuse, or mental health, it is important to approach these conversations with empathy, openness, and honesty. By navigating these discussions in a thoughtful and respectful manner, you can strengthen your relationship with your child and provide important guidance and support.

One of the most important things to keep in mind when preparing to have a difficult conversation with your child is to create a safe and non-judgmental space for them to express themselves. This means being open and receptive to their thoughts and feelings, even if they differ from your own. It is essential to listen actively to what your child has to say, without interrupting or dismissing their perspective. By demonstrating empathy and understanding, you can show your child that you value their opinions and are willing to engage in an honest and respectful dialogue.

When broaching a sensitive topic with your child, it is crucial to approach the conversation with honesty and integrity. It may be tempting to avoid difficult topics or sugarcoat the truth to protect your child from discomfort or distress, but this approach can ultimately do more harm than good. By being straightforward and transparent in your communication, you can build trust and credibility with your child, and foster a sense of mutual respect in your relationship. Remember that children are perceptive and can often sense when they are not being given the full picture, so it is important to be truthful and forthcoming in your discussions.

Another important aspect of navigating difficult conversations with your child is to be prepared and informed about the topic at hand. Before initiating a discussion, take the time to educate yourself about the issue and gather relevant information and resources to support your conversation. This can help you feel more confident and equipped to address your child's questions or concerns, and can also demonstrate to your child that you take the topic seriously and have invested time and effort in understanding it. By arming yourself with knowledge, you can avoid miscommunication or confusion, and provide accurate and helpful guidance to your child.

In addition to being well-informed, it is important to approach difficult conversations with your child with patience and understanding. Remember that these discussions can be emotionally charged and may bring up strong feelings for both you and your child. It is important to remain calm and composed, even if you are feeling anxious or upset. By modeling emotional self-regulation and resilience, you can help your child feel more secure and supported, and create a conducive environment for constructive dialogue. If necessary, take breaks during the conversation to give yourself and your child time to process emotions and recompose yourselves before continuing.

Lastly, it is important to follow up on difficult conversations with your child to ensure that they feel supported and understood. Check in with your child regularly and encourage open communication about their thoughts and feelings on the topic at hand. Maintain an ongoing dialogue with your child to address any lingering questions or concerns, and provide reassurance and guidance as needed. By following up on difficult conversations, you can show your child that you are committed to their well-being and growth, and that you are available to support them through any challenges or difficulties they may face. Remember that building a strong and trusting relationship with your child takes time and effort, but by approaching difficult conversations with empathy, openness, and honesty, you can strengthen your bond and foster a sense of mutual respect and understanding.

Chapter 4: Implementing Positive Discipline Techniques

- Using positive reinforcement to encourage good behavior

Positive reinforcement is a powerful tool in shaping behavior and encouraging positive actions and attitudes. It involves rewarding desired behaviors with something enjoyable or beneficial, which increases the likelihood of those behaviors being repeated in the future. By focusing on the positive and reinforcing good behavior, individuals are more likely to feel motivated and engaged in their actions. This technique is widely used in various settings, including education, parenting, and even in the workplace, to promote a culture of positivity and productivity.

One of the key principles of positive reinforcement is the idea of rewarding good behavior in a timely manner. This means that the reward should be given immediately after the desired behavior is exhibited, so that the individual can clearly see the connection between their actions and the positive outcome. This reinforces the behavior and strengthens the association between the behavior and the reward, making it more likely that the behavior will be repeated in the future. By providing immediate and consistent rewards for good behavior, individuals are more likely to internalize the positive actions and make them a part of their routine.

Another important aspect of positive reinforcement is the use of specific and meaningful rewards. The reward should be something that is considered valuable or enjoyable by the individual, and should be directly tied to the desired behavior. This could be anything from verbal praise and encouragement, to tangible rewards such as stickers or small prizes. By choosing rewards that are meaningful to the individual, the positive reinforcement is more likely to be effective and have a lasting impact on behavior. It is also important to vary the types of rewards given, to keep the individual engaged and motivated to continue exhibiting the desired behavior.

In addition to providing immediate and meaningful rewards, it is also important to be consistent in using positive reinforcement to encourage good behavior. This means that the reward should be given every time the desired behavior is exhibited, to reinforce the connection between the behavior and the reward. Consistency is key in building positive habits and shaping behavior, as individuals are more likely to continue engaging in positive actions if they know that they will be rewarded for doing so. By being consistent in using positive reinforcement, individuals will learn to associate the desired behavior with positive outcomes, and will be more motivated to continue exhibiting that behavior in the future.

It is also important to note that positive reinforcement should be used in conjunction with other forms of behavior management techniques, such as setting clear expectations and providing consequences for negative behavior. While positive reinforcement is a powerful tool in shaping behavior, it is not a one-size-fits-all solution and may not be effective in every situation. By combining positive reinforcement with other techniques, such as setting boundaries and providing consequences for negative behavior, individuals are more likely to learn the importance of good behavior and the consequences of their actions. By providing immediate and meaningful rewards, being consistent in rewarding good behavior, and using positive reinforcement in conjunction with other behavior management techniques, individuals can be motivated to exhibit positive actions and attitudes. Positive reinforcement is a powerful tool that can be used in various settings to promote positive behavior and create a culture of positivity and productivity.

- Setting clear and consistent boundaries for your child

Setting clear and consistent boundaries for your child is essential for their development and well-being. Boundaries provide children with a sense of security, structure, and predictability in their lives. They also help children learn appropriate behavior, develop self-control, and understand consequences for their actions. By establishing boundaries, parents can create a safe and nurturing environment for their children to grow and thrive.

One of the key aspects of setting boundaries for your child is consistency. Consistency means enforcing the same rules and expectations consistently, regardless of the situation or context. When boundaries are inconsistent, children can become confused and unsure of what is expected of them. This can lead to behavioral problems, defiance, and a lack of respect for authority. Consistent boundaries help children understand the consequences of their actions and provide a framework for them to navigate the world around them.

It is important for parents to establish clear and age-appropriate boundaries for their children. Boundaries should be communicated in a positive and constructive manner, using language that is easy for children to understand. By setting clear boundaries, parents can help children understand what is expected of them and why certain behaviors are not acceptable. This can prevent misunderstandings and conflicts and promote positive communication between parents and children.

When setting boundaries for your child, it is important to be firm but fair. Boundaries should be reasonable and realistic, taking into account the child's age, development, and individual needs. It is important to set boundaries that are achievable and appropriate for the child's level of understanding and maturity. By being firm but fair, parents can establish a sense of authority and respect without resorting to harsh or punitive measures.

Consistency is key when it comes to enforcing boundaries. Children need to know that the rules are non-negotiable and will be enforced consistently. By following through on consequences for breaking boundaries, parents can teach children the importance of accountability and responsibility. Consistency also helps children develop self-discipline and self-control, as they learn that there are consequences for their actions.

It is important for parents to be proactive when setting boundaries for their children. This means anticipating potential challenges and setting clear expectations in advance. By discussing and reinforcing boundaries before problems arise, parents can help children understand what is expected of them and how to behave in various situations. Proactive boundary-setting also helps parents establish a positive and supportive relationship with their children, as they work together to create a safe and nurturing environment. Boundaries provide children with a sense of security, structure, and predictability, helping them navigate the world around them. By establishing clear and age-appropriate boundaries, being firm but fair, and enforcing boundaries consistently, parents can create a safe and nurturing environment for their children to grow and thrive. Proactive boundary-setting helps children develop self-discipline and self-control, as they learn the importance of accountability and responsibility. With clear boundaries in place, children can develop positive behavior and healthy relationships, setting them up for success in the future.

Chapter 5: Building a Strong Relationship with Your Child

- Fostering trust and emotional connection with your child

Building trust and emotional connection with your child is essential for their overall well-being and development. When children feel secure and loved, they are more likely to thrive academically, socially, and emotionally. As a parent, there are several strategies you can implement to foster a strong bond with your child that is rooted in trust and emotional connection.

First and foremost, it is important to create a safe and nurturing environment for your child. This means setting boundaries and guidelines that are clear and consistent, while also being empathetic and understanding of your child's needs and emotions. Consistent routines and expectations help children feel secure and know what to expect, which can reduce anxiety and confusion. By creating a safe and predictable environment, you are laying the foundation for trust and emotional connection to flourish.

Communication is another key component in building trust and emotional connection with your child. Being an active listener and validating your child's feelings shows them that their thoughts and emotions are important and valued. Encouraging open and honest communication also helps foster a sense of trust between you and your child, as they know they can come to you with any concerns or problems they may have. It is important to create a safe space for your child to express themselves without fear of judgment or retribution.

Showing empathy and understanding towards your child's emotions is crucial in building trust and emotional connection. Acknowledge their feelings, even if you may not agree with them, and validate their experiences. By demonstrating empathy and understanding, you are showing your child that you care about their well-being and are there to support them through their struggles. This helps build a sense of trust between you and your child, as they know they can rely on you for comfort and guidance during difficult times.

Spending quality time with your child is another important way to foster trust and emotional connection. Engaging in activities together, such as playing games, reading books, or going for walks, helps strengthen the bond between you and your child. Quality time allows for opportunities to connect on a deeper level and build shared experiences that create lasting memories. It is important to be present and fully engaged during these moments, showing your child that they are your top priority and that you value their company.

Respect is a fundamental component in building trust and emotional connection with your child. Respecting your child's autonomy and individuality helps them feel valued and respected as individuals. By honoring their opinions and choices, you are showing your child that their voice matters and that they can trust you to respect their desires and boundaries. Respect also means modeling positive behavior and treating your child with kindness and empathy, even during moments of conflict or disagreement. Respecting your child as a unique individual helps build a strong foundation of trust and emotional connection.

To bring to a close, it is important to be a positive role model for your child in order to foster trust and emotional connection. Children learn by example, so demonstrating the values and behaviors you want to instill in your child is crucial. Show kindness, empathy, and respect towards others, and your child will learn to do the same. Be honest and transparent in your communication, and your child will come to trust you and feel emotionally connected to you. By modeling positive behavior and values, you are teaching your child important life skills that will help them navigate the world with confidence and integrity. By creating a safe and nurturing environment, prioritizing communication and empathy, spending quality time together, showing respect, and being a positive role model, you can foster a strong bond with your child that is rooted in trust and emotional connection. Investing in your relationship with your child pays off in the long run, as it helps them develop into confident, secure, and resilient individuals who are capable of forming healthy relationships and navigating life's challenges with grace.

- Creating special moments for bonding with your child

Creating special moments for bonding with your child is crucial for fostering a strong and healthy relationship. In today's fast-paced world, it can be easy to get caught up in the hustle and bustle of daily life and overlook the importance of spending quality time with your child. However, taking the time to create special moments can have a lasting impact on your child's development and overall well-being.

One of the most effective ways to create special moments for bonding with your child is to carve out dedicated one-on-one time with them. This could be as simple as setting aside a few hours each week to do an activity that you both enjoy, such as going for a walk in the park, baking cookies together, or playing a board game. By prioritizing this time with your child, you show them that they are important to you and that you value your relationship with them.

Another way to create special moments for bonding with your child is to engage in activities that allow for open communication and connection. This could involve having regular conversations with your child about their day, their thoughts and feelings, and any challenges they may be facing. By creating a safe and supportive environment for your child to express themselves, you can strengthen the bond between you and foster a sense of trust and understanding.

Additionally, participating in activities that promote teamwork and cooperation can be a great way to create special bonding moments with your child. This could involve working together to complete a puzzle, build a model, or plant a garden. By collaborating on a project or task, you can strengthen your relationship with your child and teach them important skills such as communication, problem-solving, and teamwork.

It's also important to be present and fully engaged during these special bonding moments with your child. Put away distractions such as phones, tablets, or the television, and focus on spending quality time together. Show genuine interest in your child's thoughts and feelings, and be an active listener. By giving your full attention to your child, you demonstrate that you value and appreciate the time you spend together.

In addition to creating special moments for bonding with your child, it's also important to prioritize self-care and self-compassion as a parent. Taking care of yourself and making time for your own needs can help you show up as the best version of yourself for your child. Remember that it's okay to ask for help when you need it, and to set boundaries to ensure that you have the time and space to recharge. By prioritizing one-on-one time, open communication, teamwork, and presence, you can strengthen the bond between you and your child and create lasting memories that will benefit both of you for years to come. Remember to prioritize self-care as a parent, and to show yourself the same love and compassion that you show your child. By investing in these special moments, you can create a strong foundation for a loving and supportive relationship with your child.

Chapter 6: Nurturing Your Child's Emotional Intelligence

- Teaching your child how to recognize and manage their emotions

Teaching children how to recognize and manage their emotions is a crucial aspect of their overall development and well-being. Emotional intelligence is a key component of social and emotional competence, which is essential for success in school, relationships, and life in general. By helping children understand and navigate their emotions, parents can equip them with valuable skills that will serve them well in various aspects of their lives.

One of the first steps in teaching children how to recognize and manage their emotions is helping them understand what emotions are and how they manifest themselves. Emotions are complex and varied, and children may not always have the vocabulary or the cognitive ability to articulate what they are feeling. As a parent, you can help your child recognize and name their emotions by talking to them about how they are feeling, asking them about their emotions, and validating their feelings. By providing a safe and supportive environment for your child to express themselves, you can lay the foundation for healthy emotional development.

In addition to helping children recognize and name their emotions, it is important to teach them how to manage those emotions in a healthy and constructive way. Children often struggle with regulating their emotions, as their developing brains may not yet have the capacity to effectively control their impulses and reactions. As a parent, you can help your child develop emotional regulation skills by teaching them coping strategies, such as deep breathing exercises, mindfulness techniques, and positive self-talk. By providing guidance and modeling positive emotional regulation behaviors, you can help your child learn how to manage their emotions in a healthy and adaptive manner.

Another important aspect of teaching children how to recognize and manage their emotions is helping them understand the connection between thoughts, feelings, and behaviors. Children may not always be aware of the ways in which their thoughts can influence their emotions and actions. By helping your child identify and challenge negative or unhelpful thoughts, you can empower them to change their emotional responses and behaviors. For example, if your child is feeling anxious about an upcoming test, you can help them reframe their thoughts in a more positive and realistic way, which can help alleviate their anxiety and improve their performance.

It is also important to teach children the value of empathy and perspective-taking in managing their emotions. Empathy is the ability to understand and share the feelings of others, and it plays a crucial role in building positive relationships and resolving conflicts. By encouraging your child to consider the perspectives and feelings of others, you can help them develop a sense of empathy and compassion, which can in turn help them regulate their own emotions more effectively. Teaching children to put themselves in others' shoes can also help them gain a broader perspective on their own emotions and behaviors, enabling them to respond more thoughtfully and empathetically in social situations. By helping children understand and name their emotions, develop emotional regulation skills, connect their thoughts, feelings, and behaviors, and cultivate empathy and perspective-taking, parents can empower their children to navigate their emotions in a healthy and constructive way. By modeling positive emotional regulation behaviors and providing support and guidance, parents can equip their children with valuable skills that will serve them well throughout their lives.

- Helping your child develop empathy and social skills

Developing empathy and social skills in children is paramount in preparing them for success in both their personal and professional lives. Empathy is the ability to understand and share the feelings of others, while social skills are the behaviors and communication strategies that allow individuals to interact effectively with others. By fostering empathy and social skills in children, parents can help them build positive relationships, navigate social situations, and contribute to a more compassionate and inclusive society.

There are several strategies that parents can employ to help their children develop empathy and social skills. One of the most important ways to foster empathy in children is by modeling empathetic behavior yourself. Show your child how to express concern for others, listen actively, and respond with kindness and understanding. By demonstrating empathy in your own interactions with others, you are providing a powerful example for your child to follow.

Another important way to nurture empathy in children is to encourage perspective-taking. Help your child understand that people may have different thoughts, feelings, and experiences than they do, and that it is important to consider these perspectives when interacting with others. Encouraging your child to imagine how someone else might be feeling in a given situation can help them develop a more empathetic mindset.

In addition to fostering empathy, it is important for parents to help their children develop social skills that will enable them to navigate social interactions successfully. One key aspect of social skills is effective communication. Teach your child how to express themselves clearly and respectfully, listen actively to others, and ask questions to show interest and understanding. Encourage your child to practice these communication skills in a variety of settings, such as at home, at school, and with friends.

Another essential social skill for children to develop is the ability to form and maintain positive relationships. Help your child understand the importance of being kind, considerate, and supportive in their interactions with others. Encourage them to reach out to peers, show empathy, and offer help when needed. By helping your child build strong and positive relationships, you are setting the stage for them to thrive socially and emotionally.

It is also important for parents to teach their children how to navigate social conflicts and challenges. Help your child understand that conflicts are a natural part of relationships, and teach them strategies for resolving disagreements peacefully and constructively. Encourage your child to communicate openly and honestly with others, express their feelings calmly, and work together to find solutions that are mutually beneficial. By equipping your child with these conflict resolution skills, you are helping them build strong and resilient relationships that will serve them well throughout their lives. By modeling empathetic behavior, encouraging perspective-taking, teaching effective communication, fostering positive relationships, and providing conflict resolution strategies, parents can play a critical role in helping their children build the skills and abilities they need to thrive in a diverse and interconnected world. By investing time and energy in nurturing empathy and social skills in their children, parents can help them become compassionate, confident, and socially adept individuals who are capable of making a positive impact on the world around them.

Chapter 7: Encouraging Independence and Responsibility

- Empowering your child to make decisions and take responsibility

One of the key aspects of parenting is empowering your child to make decisions and take responsibility. This is important for their personal development and growth, as it allows them to learn valuable life skills and independence. By giving your child the opportunity to make decisions and take responsibility for their actions, you are helping them to build confidence and self-esteem. It also teaches them the importance of accountability and the consequences of their choices.

Empowering your child to make decisions and take responsibility starts with providing them with opportunities to do so. This could be as simple as letting them choose what to wear, what activities to participate in, or what books to read. By giving them the freedom to make choices, you are showing them that their opinions and preferences are valued. It also allows them to practice critical thinking and problem-solving skills, as they weigh the pros and cons of different options.

It is important to guide your child in the decision-making process, without micromanaging or dictating their choices. Encourage them to think about the potential outcomes of their decisions and to consider the feelings and needs of others. Help them to set goals and make a plan of action to achieve those goals. By offering support and guidance, you are empowering your child to take ownership of their decisions and actions.

As your child begins to take on more responsibility, be sure to provide positive reinforcement and praise for their efforts. Acknowledge their accomplishments and celebrate their successes, no matter how small. This will help to boost their self-confidence and motivate them to continue making positive choices. It is also important to address any mistakes or challenges that arise along the way, as these provide valuable learning opportunities. Encourage your child to reflect on their decisions and assess what they could have done differently.

Another important aspect of empowering your child to make decisions and take responsibility is teaching them the value of accountability. Help them to understand that every choice they make has consequences, both positive and negative. Encourage them to take ownership of their actions and to apologize or make amends when necessary. By holding them accountable for their behavior, you are teaching them the importance of integrity and honesty.

It is also important to model responsible decision-making and accountability in your own actions. Show your child how you weigh options, set goals, and take ownership of your choices. By setting a positive example, you are demonstrating the importance of personal responsibility and showing your child how to navigate the challenges of decision-making. By providing them with opportunities to make choices and guiding them in the decision-making process, you are helping them to develop important life skills and independence. Encourage positive behavior and hold them accountable for their actions, while also providing support and guidance along the way. By fostering a sense of responsibility and accountability, you are setting your child up for success in all areas of their life.

- Teaching your child important life skills for independence

Teaching your child important life skills for independence is crucial in setting them up for success in the future. As parents, it is our responsibility to instill in our children the abilities they need to navigate the world on their own. From basic tasks like cooking and cleaning to more advanced skills like managing finances and problem-solving, teaching our children these essential life skills will help them become self-sufficient and independent adults.

One important life skill that children should learn is how to cook and prepare meals for themselves. Cooking is a valuable skill that not only helps children become more self-reliant but also promotes healthy eating habits. By teaching children how to cook simple meals and follow recipes, we are giving them the tools they need to make healthy food choices and save money by eating at home. Cooking also fosters creativity and independence, as children learn to experiment with different ingredients and flavors to create delicious dishes.

Another important life skill for children to learn is how to manage their finances. Teaching children the value of money, how to budget, and how to save will set them up for financial success in the future. By giving children an allowance and encouraging them to save a portion of it, we are teaching them the importance of delayed gratification and financial responsibility. As children grow older, they can learn more advanced financial skills such as setting financial goals, investing, and managing credit. By instilling these skills early on, we are setting our children up for financial independence and stability.

Critical thinking and problem-solving are essential life skills that children should learn from a young age. By encouraging children to think critically and solve problems on their own, we are helping them become independent and self-reliant individuals. Critical thinking skills help children analyze information, make informed decisions, and solve problems effectively. By teaching children how to think critically and approach challenges with a positive mindset, we are setting them up for success in school, work, and life.

In addition to practical life skills, emotional intelligence is another important skill that children should develop. Emotional intelligence involves understanding and managing one's emotions, as well as being able to empathize with others and build healthy relationships. By teaching children how to identify and express their emotions in a healthy way, we are helping them develop self-awareness and emotional resilience. Emotional intelligence also helps children navigate social situations, build positive relationships, and resolve conflicts effectively. By fostering emotional intelligence in our children, we are giving them the tools they need to succeed in both their personal and professional lives. By instilling in our children the abilities to cook, manage finances, think critically, and develop emotional intelligence, we are helping them become self-sufficient and independent individuals. These life skills not only promote self-reliance and confidence but also help children navigate the complexities of the world with ease and grace. As parents, it is our responsibility to empower our children with the tools they need to thrive and succeed in all aspects of their lives.

Chapter 8: Guiding Your Child Through Challenges and Setbacks

- Helping your child build resilience and perseverance

Parenting is a challenging task that requires a delicate balance of nurturing and guiding our children to become resilient and persistent individuals. In today's fast-paced and competitive world, it is more important than ever to instill in our children the qualities of resilience and perseverance. These qualities not only help them navigate life's challenges and setbacks but also set them up for success in the long term. In this article, we will explore some practical strategies that parents can use to help their children build resilience and perseverance.

One of the key ways to help children build resilience and perseverance is to encourage a growth mindset. Carol Dweck, a renowned psychologist, coined the term "growth mindset" to describe the belief that abilities and intelligence can be developed through effort and hard work. Children with a growth mindset are more likely to view challenges as opportunities for growth and learning, rather than as insurmountable obstacles. As parents, we can cultivate a growth mindset in our children by praising their efforts and perseverance, rather than just their intelligence or talents. By emphasizing the process of learning and growth, rather than just the end result, we can help our children develop a resilient attitude towards setbacks and failures.

Another important way to help children build resilience and perseverance is to teach them problem-solving skills. Resilient individuals are able to effectively navigate and overcome challenges by breaking them down into manageable parts and coming up with practical solutions. As parents, we can help our children develop their problem-solving skills by encouraging them to think critically and creatively, and by providing them with the support and guidance they need to tackle difficult tasks. By teaching our children how to approach problems with a positive and proactive mindset, we can help them build the resilience and perseverance they need to succeed in life.

In addition to fostering a growth mindset and teaching problem-solving skills, parents can also help their children build resilience and perseverance by modeling these qualities themselves. Children learn by example, and observing how their parents cope with challenges and setbacks can have a powerful impact on their own attitudes and behaviors. As parents, it is important to demonstrate resilience and perseverance in our own lives, whether it is by taking on new challenges, bouncing back from failure, or persevering in the face of adversity. By modeling these qualities for our children, we can inspire them to develop the same traits in themselves.

Furthermore, building strong relationships and support networks can also help children develop resilience and perseverance. Studies have shown that individuals who have strong social support systems are better able to cope with stress and adversity, and are more likely to bounce back from setbacks. As parents, we can help our children build strong relationships with family members, friends, teachers, and other supportive adults who can provide guidance, encouragement, and emotional support during difficult times. By nurturing these relationships and helping our children cultivate a sense of belonging and connection, we can help them develop the resilience and perseverance they need to thrive in the face of life's challenges.

To bring to a close, it is important for parents to recognize that building resilience and perseverance is a gradual process that requires patience, persistence, and consistency. Children may struggle with setbacks and failures along the way, and it is important for parents to provide them with the encouragement and support they need to keep going. By acknowledging their efforts and celebrating their progress, we can help our children develop the confidence and motivation they need to persevere in the face of adversity. In the end, by following these strategies and supporting our children with love and understanding, we can help them build the resilience and perseverance they need to thrive in life.

- Supporting your child through difficult times

Supporting a child through difficult times can be a challenging and emotionally taxing experience for parents or caregivers. It is crucial to understand that children may express their emotions and cope with stress in various ways, which may sometimes be different from how adults do. As caregivers, it is important to provide a safe and supportive environment for children to express their feelings and process their emotions. By being present and attentive, caregivers can help children navigate through difficult times and develop healthy coping mechanisms.

One of the first steps in supporting a child through difficult times is to create an open and non-judgmental environment for them to share their feelings. Children may feel frightened or overwhelmed by their emotions, and it is essential to let them know that it is okay to express themselves. Caregivers should actively listen to their child's concerns and validate their feelings, even if they may seem trivial or insignificant. By showing empathy and understanding, caregivers can help children feel supported and encourage them to open up about their struggles.

In addition to creating a safe space for their child to talk about their feelings, caregivers should also provide reassurance and comfort during difficult times. Children may feel scared or uncertain about the future, and it is important for caregivers to offer words of encouragement and support. Reassuring children that they are loved and cared for can help them feel secure and build their resilience in the face of adversity. Caregivers can also emphasize the importance of self-care and teach children healthy coping strategies, such as deep breathing exercises or mindfulness techniques, to help manage their stress.

Furthermore, caregivers should seek professional help if they notice signs of prolonged distress or behavioral changes in their child. While it is normal for children to experience occasional periods of sadness or anxiety, persistent symptoms of depression or anxiety may require professional intervention. It is essential for caregivers to be proactive in addressing their child's mental health needs and seek support from a qualified therapist or counselor if necessary. By taking a proactive approach to their child's emotional well-being, caregivers can help ensure that their child receives the necessary support and resources to cope with difficult times.

Moreover, caregivers should prioritize their own self-care and well-being to better support their child through difficult times. It is common for caregivers to feel overwhelmed or stressed when their child is going through a challenging situation, and it is important to practice self-care strategies to maintain their own mental health. Taking time for oneself, engaging in enjoyable activities, and seeking support from friends or family members can help caregivers recharge and stay resilient in the face of adversity. By prioritizing their own well-being, caregivers can set a positive example for their child and show them the importance of self-care during difficult times. Caregivers play a critical role in helping children navigate through challenging situations and develop healthy coping mechanisms. By creating a safe and supportive environment, providing reassurance and comfort, seeking professional help when needed, and prioritizing self-care, caregivers can help their child build resilience and thrive in the face of adversity. It is essential for caregivers to be proactive in addressing their child's emotional well-being and to show them love and support during difficult times. By working together, caregivers and children can overcome obstacles and emerge stronger and more resilient.

Chapter 9: Creating a Positive and Supportive Environment

- Cultivating a loving and nurturing home environment

Creating a loving and nurturing home environment is crucial for the well-being and development of every member of the household. From young children to adults, the atmosphere in which we live plays a significant role in shaping our thoughts, feelings, and behaviors. A warm and supportive home environment can foster a sense of security, build strong relationships, and promote emotional growth. In contrast, a cold or hostile home environment can lead to feelings of anxiety, insecurity, and dissatisfaction. Cultivating a loving and nurturing home environment requires intentional effort and commitment, but the rewards can be immense.

One of the key components of a loving and nurturing home environment is effective communication. Open and honest communication among family members allows for the expression of thoughts, feelings, and concerns in a safe and respectful manner. Listening attentively to each other, expressing empathy, and offering support are essential skills for effective communication within the family. Setting aside time for regular family meetings or discussions can help create a sense of connection and understanding among family members. By fostering a culture of open communication, family members can build trust, resolve conflicts, and strengthen their relationships.

Another important aspect of cultivating a loving and nurturing home environment is the promotion of positive relationships within the family. Building strong and healthy relationships among family members requires patience, respect, and mutual support. Encouraging teamwork, collaboration, and shared responsibilities can foster a sense of unity and belonging within the family. Showing appreciation, practicing forgiveness, and expressing love and affection can also contribute to building strong bonds among family members. By prioritizing positive relationships and creating a sense of belonging, family members can feel valued, supported, and connected to each other.

Creating a loving and nurturing home environment also involves setting clear boundaries and expectations. Establishing boundaries helps to create a sense of structure, predictability, and security within the family. Consistent rules and expectations provide guidance for behavior, promote accountability, and create a sense of order within the home. By setting boundaries and expectations, family members can develop a sense of respect for themselves and others, as well as an understanding of appropriate behavior. Clear communication of boundaries and expectations can also help prevent conflicts, misunderstandings, and tension within the family.

In addition to communication, relationships, and boundaries, the physical environment of the home also plays a significant role in creating a loving and nurturing atmosphere. A well-maintained, clean, and organized home can promote a sense of calm, comfort, and security for family members. Creating a space that is welcoming, inviting, and peaceful can help reduce stress, promote relaxation, and enhance overall well-being. By taking care of the physical environment of the home, family members can create a sense of pride, ownership, and belonging, which can contribute to a positive and nurturing atmosphere. By fostering open and honest communication, positive relationships, clear boundaries, and a well-maintained home, family members can create a sense of security, support, and connection. A loving and nurturing home environment provides the foundation for emotional growth, healthy relationships, and overall well-being for every member of the family. By prioritizing the well-being of the family and investing time and energy into creating a positive home environment, family members can enjoy a sense of peace, happiness, and fulfillment in their daily lives.

- Creating routines and structures to support your child's growth

As parents, we play a crucial role in shaping our children's development and growth. One way to support this growth is by creating routines and structures that provide stability and predictability in their daily lives. Routines help children feel secure and confident, as they know what to expect and can anticipate what will happen next. This sense of predictability can help reduce anxiety and promote a sense of well-being in children. Additionally, routines can also teach children important skills such as time management, organization, and responsibility.

Creating routines and structures for your child involves establishing consistent daily habits and patterns that help guide their behavior and activities. This can include setting regular bedtimes and wake-up times, establishing meal times, scheduling homework and study time, and incorporating regular exercise and playtime into their daily routine. By providing a framework for your child's day, you can help them develop important self-regulation skills and promote healthy habits that will support their growth and development.

One important aspect of creating routines and structures for your child is to involve them in the process. Giving children a sense of ownership and autonomy in establishing their routines can help them feel more motivated and engaged in following them. You can involve your child in setting goals and expectations for their daily routines, and work together to create a schedule that works best for them. This can also help children develop important decision-making and problem-solving skills, as they learn to prioritize and manage their time effectively.

It is also important to be flexible and adaptive when creating routines and structures for your child. Children's needs and preferences can change over time, so it's important to regularly reassess and adjust their routines as needed. This can involve tweaking schedules, incorporating new activities or interests, or making accommodations for special events or circumstances. By being responsive to your child's changing needs and preferences, you can ensure that their routines continue to support their growth and development in a positive and effective way.

In addition to creating daily routines and structures, it's also important to establish larger-scale routines and structures that provide a sense of continuity and stability for your child. This can include setting regular family routines such as weekly family meals, weekend outings, or holiday traditions. By establishing these larger-scale routines, you can create a sense of cohesion and connection within your family, and provide your child with a strong foundation of support and stability as they navigate the ups and downs of daily life. By establishing consistent daily habits and patterns, involving your child in the process, being flexible and adaptive, and setting larger-scale routines, you can provide your child with the support and guidance they need to thrive and reach their full potential. By prioritizing routines and structures that promote stability, predictability, and autonomy, you can help your child develop important skills and habits that will serve them well throughout their life.

Chapter 10: Promoting a Healthy Lifestyle for Your Child

- Encouraging healthy eating habits and physical activity

Healthy eating and regular physical activity are key components of leading a healthy lifestyle. By making small changes to our daily habits, we can improve our quality of life and reduce the risk of developing health problems such as obesity, heart disease, diabetes, and certain types of cancer.

One of the first steps to encourage healthy eating habits is to educate individuals on the importance of consuming a balanced diet rich in fruits, vegetables, whole grains, lean proteins, and healthy fats. A balanced diet provides the necessary nutrients that our bodies need to function properly and stay healthy. By including a variety of foods from all the food groups in our meals, we can ensure that we are getting the essential vitamins, minerals, and antioxidants that our bodies need to thrive.

In addition to eating a balanced diet, it is important to pay attention to portion sizes and practice mindful eating. Portion control is key to maintaining a healthy weight and preventing overeating. By listening to our body's hunger and fullness cues, we can avoid mindless eating and make healthier choices when it comes to food. Eating slowly, savoring each bite, and avoiding distractions such as watching TV or eating on the go can help us to be more mindful of what we are eating and how much we are consuming.

Another important aspect of encouraging healthy eating habits is to promote home-cooked meals and reduce the consumption of processed and fast foods. Cooking at home allows us to have control over the ingredients that we use in our meals and can help us to make healthier choices. By preparing meals from scratch, we can avoid added sugars, unhealthy fats, and preservatives that are often found in pre-packaged foods. Additionally, cooking at home can be a fun and rewarding experience that can bring families together and foster a greater appreciation for wholesome, nutritious foods.

In addition to healthy eating habits, regular physical activity is crucial for maintaining a healthy lifestyle and preventing chronic diseases. Physical activity has numerous benefits for our physical and mental health, including reducing the risk of obesity, heart disease, diabetes, and depression.

To encourage physical activity, it is important to find activities that are enjoyable and fit into our daily routine. Whether it's going for a walk, riding a bike, dancing, swimming, or practicing yoga, finding an activity that we enjoy can make it easier to stay motivated and committed to regular exercise. It is also important to set realistic goals and create a plan that works for our individual schedule and fitness level. By starting small and gradually increasing the intensity and duration of our workouts, we can build a sustainable exercise routine that we can maintain over the long term.

In addition to finding enjoyable activities, it is important to incorporate physical activity into our daily routine and make it a priority. This can include taking the stairs instead of the elevator, parking further away from the entrance, or scheduling regular breaks during the workday to stretch and move around. It is never too late to start making healthier choices and take control of our health. By prioritizing our health and well-being, we can enjoy a higher quality of life and reduce the risk of developing preventable health problems.

- Teaching your child the importance of self-care and well-being

By instilling these values at a young age, you are providing them with the tools they need to prioritize their physical, emotional, and mental well-being throughout their lives. Self-care is not just about taking care of oneself physically through proper diet and exercise, but also about nurturing one's emotional and mental health through activities that promote relaxation, stress reduction, and self-reflection.

One of the most important aspects of teaching your child about self-care is leading by example. Children learn by observing the behavior of those around them, so it is crucial that you model healthy self-care practices in your own life. This means taking time for yourself to recharge and engage in activities that bring you joy and relaxation. By showing your child that taking care of yourself is important, you are setting a positive example for them to follow.

Another key aspect of teaching your child about self-care is helping them develop a routine that includes activities that promote well-being. This can include setting aside time each day for physical activity, mindfulness practices, and relaxation techniques. By incorporating these activities into their daily routine, you are helping your child develop healthy habits that will benefit them in the long run.

In addition to physical self-care, it is important to also teach your child about the importance of emotional well-being. This includes helping them recognize and manage their emotions in a healthy way, as well as promoting positive self-esteem and self-acceptance. Encouraging your child to express their feelings and thoughts openly and honestly can help them develop emotional resilience and coping skills.

When teaching your child about self-care, it is important to emphasize the importance of balance. This means finding a healthy equilibrium between taking care of oneself and attending to the needs of others. Teaching your child to prioritize their own well-being while also being mindful of the needs of others will help them develop a sense of empathy and compassion towards themselves and others.

Furthermore, it is important to teach your child about the importance of setting boundaries and saying no when needed. By empowering your child to prioritize their own well-being and set limits on their time and energy, you are helping them develop assertiveness and self-advocacy skills that will serve them well in all aspects of their lives. By modeling healthy practices, helping them develop a routine that includes activities that promote well-being, emphasizing the importance of emotional well-being, teaching them about balance, and empowering them to set boundaries, you are equipping your child with the tools they need to prioritize their own self-care throughout their lives. Remember, self-care is not selfish – it is a necessary component of living a fulfilling and balanced life.

Chapter 11: Managing Technology and Screen Time

- Setting limits on screen time and monitoring content

In today's digital age, the proliferation of screens in our daily lives poses a unique challenge for parents and caregivers. With the increasing prevalence of smartphones, tablets, computers, and televisions, it has become more important than ever to set limits on screen time and monitor the content that children are exposed to. While screens can provide incredible educational opportunities and entertainment, excessive use can have negative effects on children's physical and mental health.

Setting limits on screen time is essential to ensure that children are not spending excessive amounts of time in front of screens. The American Academy of Pediatrics recommends that children aged 2 to 5 should have no more than one hour of screen time per day, while older children should have consistent limits on their screen time. By enforcing these limits, parents can help prevent children from developing unhealthy screen habits and ensure that they are engaging in a variety of activities that promote physical and mental well-being.

Monitoring the content that children are exposed to is equally important in this digital age. With the vast amount of content available online, children can easily access inappropriate or harmful material if left unsupervised. Parents should take an active role in monitoring the content their children are consuming, whether it be through parental controls on devices or by having open conversations about the importance of consuming age-appropriate content. By being vigilant about the content children are exposed to, parents can help prevent potential negative effects on children's mental and emotional development.

In addition to setting limits on screen time and monitoring content, it is important for parents to model healthy screen habits for their children. Children learn by example, so it is crucial for parents to demonstrate responsible screen use by limiting their own screen time and engaging in offline activities with their children. By setting a positive example, parents can instill healthy screen habits in their children and help them develop a balanced approach to technology use.

It is also important to create a supportive and open dialogue with children about screen time and content monitoring. Parents should communicate the reasons behind setting limits on screen time and monitoring content, and involve children in the decision-making process. By explaining the importance of balancing screen time with other activities and discussing the potential risks of consuming inappropriate content, parents can empower children to make informed choices about their screen use. By enforcing consistent limits on screen time, monitoring the content children are exposed to, modeling healthy screen habits, and fostering open communication about screen use, parents can help children develop a healthy relationship with technology. Ultimately, by taking an active role in managing children's screen time and content consumption, parents can promote their children's well-being and set them up for success in an increasingly digital world.

- Promoting healthy tech habits and fostering digital literacy

In today's digital age, promoting healthy tech habits and fostering digital literacy has become more important than ever. With the constant advancement of technology and the increasing reliance on digital devices for communication, work, and leisure, it is essential that individuals develop a strong understanding of how to use technology in a responsible and mindful way. In this essay, we will explore the benefits of promoting healthy tech habits and fostering digital literacy, as well as provide practical tips and strategies for achieving these goals.

One of the key benefits of promoting healthy tech habits and fostering digital literacy is the ability to use technology in a way that enhances our overall well-being. By developing an understanding of how to use technology in a balanced and mindful way, individuals can avoid the negative effects of excessive screen time, such as eye strain, poor posture, and reduced quality of sleep. Additionally, by fostering digital literacy, individuals can enhance their critical thinking skills, problem-solving abilities, and overall confidence when using technology.

Another important benefit of promoting healthy tech habits and fostering digital literacy is the ability to navigate the digital world safely and securely. With the increasing prevalence of online scams, cyberbullying, and data breaches, it is essential that individuals have the knowledge and skills to protect themselves and their personal information while using digital devices. By promoting healthy tech habits and fostering digital literacy, individuals can learn how to identify and avoid online threats, as well as develop strategies for protecting their privacy and security online.

Furthermore, promoting healthy tech habits and fostering digital literacy can also lead to increased productivity and efficiency in both personal and professional settings. When individuals have a strong understanding of how to use technology effectively, they can streamline their workflow, communicate more efficiently with others, and access information quickly and easily. By developing good tech habits and digital literacy skills, individuals can become more organized, focused, and productive in all aspects of their lives.

To promote healthy tech habits and foster digital literacy, there are several practical tips and strategies that individuals can implement in their daily lives. One important tip is to set boundaries around technology use, such as designating specific times of day for checking email or social media, and sticking to these boundaries to avoid the negative effects of excessive screen time. Another tip is to prioritize digital skills development by taking online courses, attending workshops, or participating in digital literacy programs to enhance one's knowledge and proficiency with technology.

Additionally, individuals can prioritize their physical health while using technology by practicing good posture, taking breaks from screens regularly, and adjusting screen brightness and settings to reduce eye strain. It is also important for individuals to stay informed about the latest trends and developments in technology, as well as to be aware of potential risks and threats in the digital world. By staying informed and educated, individuals can make more informed decisions about their tech use and better protect themselves online. By developing a strong understanding of how to use technology responsibly, safely, and efficiently, individuals can enhance their overall well-being, productivity, and security in the digital world. By following practical tips and strategies for promoting healthy tech habits and fostering digital literacy, individuals can take charge of their tech use and become more empowered and confident users of technology.

Chapter 12: Fostering Creativity and Imagination

- Providing opportunities for creative expression and exploration

Providing opportunities for creative expression and exploration is essential in promoting personal growth and development for individuals of all ages. Creativity is a fundamental aspect of human intelligence and is a powerful tool for problem-solving, innovation, and self-expression. By encouraging individuals to explore their creativity through various mediums such as art, music, writing, and performance, we can help them discover new skills, talents, and perspectives that can enrich their lives and enhance their sense of self.

One of the key benefits of providing opportunities for creative expression is that it allows individuals to tap into their inner thoughts and emotions, enabling them to process and make sense of their experiences in a unique and personal way. Through creative outlets such as painting, drawing, or writing, individuals can explore their feelings, memories, and desires in a safe and non-judgmental environment. This process of self-expression can be incredibly therapeutic and can help individuals cope with difficult emotions, gain insight into their own thoughts and behaviors, and develop a deeper understanding of themselves and the world around them.

In addition to promoting self-awareness and emotional resilience, creative expression can also foster innovation and problem-solving skills. When individuals engage in creative activities, they are encouraged to think outside the box, experiment with new ideas, and explore unconventional solutions to challenges. This process of creative exploration can help individuals develop their critical thinking abilities, enhance their problem-solving skills, and cultivate a mindset that is open to new possibilities and perspectives. By fostering a culture of creativity and innovation, we can empower individuals to think creatively, adapt to change, and thrive in an ever-evolving world.

Furthermore, providing opportunities for creative expression can also help individuals build confidence and self-esteem. When individuals engage in creative activities and explore their creative potential, they can experience a sense of accomplishment, pride, and fulfillment that can boost their confidence and self-worth. By celebrating their creative achievements and encouraging them to take risks and try new things, we can help individuals develop a positive self-image, believe in their abilities, and overcome self-doubt and fear of failure. This sense of empowerment can have a ripple effect on all aspects of their lives, from their relationships and career to their overall well-being and happiness.

In order to provide opportunities for creative expression and exploration, it is essential to create a supportive and nurturing environment that encourages individuals to take risks, make mistakes, and learn from their experiences. One way to do this is by offering a variety of creative outlets and opportunities for individuals to explore and experiment with different mediums and techniques. By providing access to art supplies, musical instruments, writing workshops, and performance spaces, we can empower individuals to discover their creative passions and talents and express themselves in a way that feels authentic and meaningful to them.

Another important aspect of fostering creativity is to provide guidance, encouragement, and constructive feedback to help individuals develop their creative skills and refine their artistic voice. By offering workshops, classes, and mentorship programs led by experienced artists and educators, we can support individuals in their creative journey, inspire them to push their boundaries, and challenge them to grow and evolve as artists and creators. This guidance and mentorship can help individuals develop their artistic abilities, unlock their creative potential, and cultivate a lifelong passion for creative expression. By encouraging individuals to explore their creativity through various mediums and channels, we can help them discover new talents, gain self-awareness, build confidence, and develop critical thinking and problem-solving skills. Through a supportive and nurturing environment that values creativity and innovation, we can empower individuals to embrace their unique voice, express themselves authentically, and create a positive impact on the world around them. Let us continue to champion creativity, celebrate diversity, and inspire others to explore their creative potential and unleash their untapped talents.

- Encouraging your child to think outside the box and problem-solve creatively

Encouraging children to think outside the box and problem-solve creatively is a crucial skill that can benefit them throughout their lives. In today's rapidly changing world, the ability to adapt and come up with innovative solutions is highly valued in the workplace and in daily life. By nurturing these skills in children from a young age, parents can help equip them with the tools they need to thrive in an increasingly complex and competitive world.

One method parents can use to encourage their child to think outside the box is to provide them with open-ended, thought-provoking questions. Instead of asking simple yes or no questions, parents can ask their child questions that require them to think critically and consider multiple perspectives. For example, instead of asking "Did you have fun at school today. " parents can ask "What was the most interesting thing you learned today and why. " This type of questioning can help children develop their analytical skills and encourage them to explore new ideas and possibilities.

Another way parents can foster creativity and problem-solving skills in their child is by exposing them to a variety of experiences and activities. By engaging in different hobbies, sports, and creative pursuits, children can learn to think creatively and approach challenges from different angles. Encouraging children to try new things and step out of their comfort zone can help them develop a growth mindset and the confidence to tackle difficult problems.

It is also important for parents to provide a supportive environment for their child to explore and experiment. This means allowing children the freedom to make mistakes and learn from them, rather than micromanaging or hovering over them. By giving children the space to explore their own ideas and solutions, parents can help build their confidence and willingness to take risks. This can lead to increased creativity and problem-solving skills in the long run.

In addition to fostering creativity and problem-solving skills, parents can also help their child develop their critical thinking abilities. Critical thinking involves analyzing information, evaluating evidence, and making reasoned judgments. By teaching children to question assumptions, consider different viewpoints, and think logically, parents can help them become more independent and analytical thinkers. This can be especially important in today's information-saturated world, where the ability to discern fact from fiction and make informed decisions is crucial.

One effective way to promote critical thinking in children is to encourage them to engage in discussions and debates. By asking children to explain their reasoning, defend their opinions, and consider alternative perspectives, parents can help them develop their analytical skills and deepen their understanding of complex issues. This can also help children learn to communicate effectively, listen to others, and respect different viewpoints – all valuable skills for problem-solving and collaboration. By nurturing their creativity, critical thinking, and problem-solving skills, parents can help equip their children with the tools they need to navigate a rapidly changing world and thrive in a variety of contexts. Through open-ended questions, diverse experiences, a supportive environment, and opportunities for critical thinking, parents can help their child develop the skills and mindset they need to become confident, adaptable, and innovative thinkers.

Chapter 13: Supporting Your Child's Academic Success

- Creating a conducive learning environment at home

In recent times, there has been a significant shift towards remote learning and homeschooling due to various reasons, such as the ongoing COVID-19 pandemic or personal preferences. This change has highlighted the importance of creating a conducive learning environment at home to support children's academic success and overall well-being. While traditional classrooms provide structure and routine, home learning environments can offer flexibility and personalized attention, making them an excellent alternative for many families. However, it is crucial to recognize that establishing a supportive and nurturing learning environment at home requires careful planning, organization, and commitment from both parents and students.

One of the key elements of creating a conducive learning environment at home is establishing a designated study space that is free from distractions and conducive to concentration. This study space should be well-lit, comfortable, and equipped with all the necessary supplies, such as books, stationery, and a computer or laptop. It is essential to set clear boundaries and establish a daily routine to help children differentiate between study time and leisure time. By creating a dedicated study area, students can better focus on their work and develop good study habits, leading to improved academic performance.

In addition to setting up a study space, it is important for parents to establish a consistent schedule that includes specific times for learning, breaks, and recreational activities. A structured routine helps children develop a sense of responsibility and discipline, promoting self-regulation and time management skills. Parents can create a daily or weekly schedule that outlines when homework should be done, when online classes or tutoring sessions will take place, and when extracurricular activities can be pursued. By following a predictable routine, children can better manage their time and prioritize their tasks, leading to increased productivity and reduced stress.

Another crucial aspect of creating a conducive learning environment at home is fostering a positive and supportive atmosphere that encourages children to engage with their studies and explore new ideas. Parents should provide encouragement, praise, and constructive feedback to motivate their children and boost their confidence. Creating a safe and nurturing environment where mistakes are seen as opportunities for growth can help children develop a growth mindset and a love for learning. By fostering a supportive atmosphere at home, parents can help their children build resilience, develop problem-solving skills, and cultivate a lifelong passion for education.

Furthermore, parents can enhance the home learning environment by incorporating technology and interactive learning tools into their children's education. With the rise of digital learning platforms and resources, parents can supplement traditional textbooks and classroom instruction with online tutorials, educational apps, and interactive games. These tools can help children stay engaged, make learning more accessible and enjoyable, and cater to different learning styles and preferences. By leveraging technology and incorporating digital resources into their children's education, parents can create a dynamic and interactive learning environment that promotes creativity, critical thinking, and collaboration. By establishing a designated study space, setting a consistent schedule, fostering a positive atmosphere, and integrating technology into their education, parents can create a supportive and enriching environment that empowers their children to reach their full potential. With dedication, organization, and a commitment to lifelong learning, parents can create a home learning environment that cultivates curiosity, self-discipline, and a thirst for knowledge in their children. By working together to create a conducive learning environment at home, families can provide a solid foundation for their children's academic and personal growth, preparing them for success in school and beyond.

- Collaborating with educators and tutors to support your child's learning

Collaborating with educators and tutors is incredibly important in supporting your child's learning and academic success. As a parent, you play a crucial role in your child's education by working closely with teachers and tutors to create a supportive learning environment both at home and in the classroom. By building strong relationships with these professionals, you can gain valuable insights into your child's academic strengths and areas for improvement, and work together to develop personalized strategies to help them reach their full potential.

Effective collaboration with educators and tutors begins with open communication and a willingness to work together towards a common goal - your child's success. Establishing a positive and collaborative relationship with your child's teachers and tutors is key to creating a supportive learning environment that fosters academic growth and development. By actively engaging in conversations with these professionals, you can gain important insights into your child's academic progress, learning style, strengths, and areas for improvement. This information is crucial in helping you and your child's educators develop personalized strategies to support their learning and address any challenges they may be facing.

One of the most important aspects of collaborating with educators and tutors is staying informed and involved in your child's education. This includes attending parent-teacher conferences, keeping in touch with your child's teachers and tutors, and staying up to date on their academic progress and any challenges they may be facing. By actively participating in your child's education, you can show your child that you value their learning and are committed to helping them succeed. Additionally, by staying informed and involved, you can work together with educators and tutors to identify any areas for improvement and develop strategies to support your child's academic growth.

Collaborating with educators and tutors also involves working together to set clear goals and expectations for your child's learning. By establishing clear goals and expectations, you can create a roadmap for your child's academic progress and monitor their performance over time. Setting realistic and achievable goals with the help of educators and tutors can help motivate your child to stay focused and committed to their learning. By working together to set clear goals and expectations, you can ensure that your child is on track to meet academic milestones and reach their full potential.

In addition to setting clear goals and expectations, collaborating with educators and tutors also involves seeking out additional support and resources to help your child succeed. This may include enlisting the help of a tutor to provide individualized support in a specific subject area, accessing educational resources and materials to supplement your child's learning, or participating in workshops and seminars to learn about effective teaching strategies and techniques. By seeking out additional support and resources, you can provide your child with the tools and assistance they need to succeed academically.

Lastly, effective collaboration with educators and tutors requires ongoing communication and feedback. By regularly communicating with your child's teachers and tutors, you can stay informed about their academic progress, address any challenges they may be facing, and adjust strategies as needed to support their learning. Providing feedback to educators and tutors about your child's progress and any areas for improvement can help them tailor their teaching methods and approaches to better meet your child's individual needs. By maintaining open lines of communication and providing feedback, you can work together with educators and tutors to create a supportive learning environment that fosters academic growth and success for your child. By building strong relationships with these professionals, staying informed and involved in your child's education, setting clear goals and expectations, seeking out additional support and resources, and maintaining ongoing communication and feedback, you can create a supportive learning environment that helps your child reach their full potential. By working together with educators and tutors, you can ensure that your child receives the help and support they need to succeed academically and achieve their educational goals.

Chapter 14: Cultivating Social Skills and Relationships

- Teaching your child how to interact with peers and adults

Teaching children how to interact with peers and adults is a crucial aspect of their social development. It is important for children to learn how to communicate effectively, show respect, and build positive relationships with others. Parents play a crucial role in teaching children these skills, as they are their first and most important teachers in life.

One of the key aspects of teaching children how to interact with peers and adults is modeling positive behavior. Children learn by observing the behavior of those around them, especially their parents. Parents should demonstrate good communication skills, patience, and respect in their interactions with others, so that children can learn by example. By modeling positive behavior, parents can help children understand the importance of treating others with kindness and respect.

Another important aspect of teaching children how to interact with peers and adults is teaching them effective communication skills. Children should be encouraged to express their thoughts, feelings, and opinions in a respectful and constructive manner. Parents can help children develop these skills by listening to them attentively, encouraging them to speak up, and providing them with opportunities to engage in conversations with others. By teaching children how to communicate effectively, parents can help them build positive relationships with their peers and adults.

In addition to modeling positive behavior and teaching effective communication skills, parents can help children learn how to interact with peers and adults by providing them with opportunities to practice these skills. This can be done through activities such as playdates, group projects, and community events where children can interact with others in a safe and supportive environment. By giving children opportunities to practice their social skills, parents can help them gain confidence and become more comfortable in social situations.

It is also important for parents to teach children how to show respect and empathy towards others. Children should be taught to treat others with kindness, compassion, and understanding. Parents can help children develop these traits by encouraging them to consider the feelings and perspectives of others, and to show empathy towards those who may be different from them. By teaching children how to show respect and empathy, parents can help them build strong and positive relationships with their peers and adults. Parents play a crucial role in helping children develop the social skills they need to navigate the world around them. By modeling positive behavior, teaching effective communication skills, providing opportunities to practice these skills, and teaching respect and empathy, parents can help children build strong and positive relationships with their peers and adults. With the right guidance and support, children can learn how to interact with others in a respectful and positive manner, setting them up for success in their social interactions both now and in the future.

- Nurturing friendships and building healthy relationships

Building and nurturing friendships is an essential component of maintaining emotional well-being and overall health. It is through our relationships with others that we experience a sense of belonging, support, and companionship. Healthy relationships contribute to our happiness, reduce stress, and provide us with a sense of purpose and fulfillment. Research has shown that people with strong social connections are happier, have lower rates of anxiety and depression, and live longer, healthier lives.

One of the key aspects of nurturing friendships and building healthy relationships is effective communication. Communication is the foundation of all relationships and is essential for expressing our thoughts, feelings, and needs.

Effective communication involves active listening, empathy, and the ability to express oneself clearly and honestly. It is important to be open and authentic in our communication, as this fosters trust and deepens our connections with others. By communicating openly and honestly, we can resolve conflicts, address misunderstandings, and strengthen our bonds with friends and loved ones.

Another important aspect of nurturing friendships and building healthy relationships is setting boundaries. Boundaries help us establish clear expectations and guidelines for how we want to be treated in our relationships. Setting boundaries is crucial for maintaining our self-respect, protecting our emotional well-being, and ensuring that our relationships are balanced and mutually fulfilling. By setting boundaries, we communicate our needs and preferences to others, which helps prevent resentments, misunderstandings, and conflicts. Boundaries also help us establish healthy limits and create a sense of safety and security in our relationships.

Creating and maintaining trust is another key element of nurturing friendships and building healthy relationships. Trust is the foundation of all successful relationships and is essential for intimacy, cooperation, and mutual respect. Trust is built through consistency, honesty, reliability, and respect for boundaries. By demonstrating trustworthiness in our actions and words, we show others that we can be relied upon, which fosters deeper connections and emotional intimacy. Trust allows us to be vulnerable, communicate openly, and seek support from others, knowing that they will honor our feelings and respect our boundaries.

Showing appreciation and gratitude is another important component of nurturing friendships and building healthy relationships. Expressing gratitude and appreciation for the people in our lives helps strengthen our connections, boost our moods, and create a positive, supportive environment. By acknowledging the support, kindness, and love that others provide us, we show them that we value and cherish their presence in our lives. Expressing gratitude also helps us focus on the positive aspects of our relationships, rather than dwelling on conflicts or misunderstandings. By cultivating a mindset of gratitude, we can foster greater happiness, resilience, and emotional well-being in our relationships. By communicating effectively, setting boundaries, creating trust, and showing appreciation, we can cultivate strong, fulfilling connections with others that enrich our lives and bring us joy. Investing time and effort in our relationships is a worthwhile endeavor that pays off in improved emotional health, increased happiness, and a sense of connection and belonging. Ultimately, building and maintaining healthy relationships is an ongoing process that requires attention, effort, and care, but the rewards of deep, meaningful connections with others are well worth the investment.

Chapter 15: Encouraging a Growth Mindset in Your Child

- Promoting a positive attitude towards challenges and learning

Promoting a positive attitude towards challenges and learning is essential for personal growth and development. When individuals approach challenges with a positive mindset, they are more likely to persevere through difficult situations and overcome obstacles. This positive attitude can lead to increased motivation, resilience, and ultimately success in both academic and professional endeavors. By fostering a mindset of curiosity, optimism, and a willingness to learn from failure, individuals can cultivate a lifelong love of learning and a growth mindset that will serve them well in all aspects of their lives.

One of the key elements of promoting a positive attitude towards challenges and learning is to encourage individuals to view challenges as opportunities for growth and development. Instead of seeing obstacles as insurmountable barriers, individuals should approach challenges with a sense of curiosity and a willingness to learn from their experiences. By reframing challenges as learning opportunities, individuals can cultivate a growth mindset that fosters a sense of resilience and determination in the face of adversity. This mindset shift can make all the difference in how individuals approach and overcome challenges in their academic and professional lives.

Another important aspect of promoting a positive attitude towards challenges and learning is to emphasize the importance of optimism and a can-do attitude. When individuals believe in their ability to overcome obstacles and achieve their goals, they are more likely to persist through difficult situations and setbacks. By cultivating a sense of optimism and self-efficacy, individuals can develop the confidence and belief in their own abilities to succeed in the face of challenges.

This positive mindset can help individuals stay motivated and focused on their goals, even when faced with uncertainty or setbacks.

In addition to promoting optimism and a growth mindset, it is also important to encourage individuals to embrace failure as a natural part of the learning process. Instead of viewing failure as a sign of inadequacy or incompetence, individuals should see it as an opportunity for growth and self-improvement. By reframing failure as a learning experience, individuals can gain valuable insights into their strengths and weaknesses and use this knowledge to inform their future actions. This willingness to learn from failure can help individuals develop a sense of resilience and adaptability that will serve them well in facing future challenges.

Furthermore, promoting a positive attitude towards challenges and learning requires creating a supportive and nurturing environment that encourages individuals to take risks and step outside of their comfort zone. By providing a safe space for individuals to explore new ideas and approaches, educators and mentors can help individuals build the confidence and skills needed to tackle difficult challenges. This supportive environment can help individuals to develop a sense of self-efficacy and agency in their own learning, empowering them to take ownership of their academic and professional development.

Ultimately, promoting a positive attitude towards challenges and learning is about fostering a sense of curiosity, optimism, and resilience in individuals. By encouraging individuals to view challenges as opportunities for growth, embrace failure as a learning experience, and cultivate a growth mindset, educators and mentors can help individuals develop the skills and attitudes needed to thrive in the face of adversity. By fostering a love of learning and a willingness to take risks, individuals can build a foundation for lifelong success and personal growth. It is through these attitudes and behaviors that individuals can approach challenges with confidence, determination, and a sense of purpose, ultimately leading to greater personal and professional fulfillment.

- Encouraging perseverance and a belief in one's ability to grow and improve

Perseverance and a belief in one's ability to grow and improve are crucial components of personal and academic success. When individuals possess these qualities, they are better equipped to navigate challenges, overcome obstacles, and reach their full potential. Encouraging perseverance and a growth mindset can have a profound impact on an individual's academic performance, career progression, and overall well-being.

One of the key ways to encourage perseverance is to provide support and guidance to individuals as they work towards their goals. This can come in the form of mentorship, coaching, or simply being a listening ear. By offering encouragement and motivation, individuals are more likely to stay determined and focused, even in the face of setbacks or adversity. It is important to remind individuals that setbacks are a natural part of the learning process and that they should not be viewed as failures, but rather as opportunities for growth and improvement.

Another important aspect of encouraging perseverance is to set realistic and achievable goals. By breaking down larger goals into smaller, more manageable tasks, individuals can build momentum and stay motivated throughout the journey. It is also important to celebrate small wins along the way, as this can help boost confidence and reinforce the belief that progress is being made. By setting clear goals and tracking progress, individuals can stay accountable and motivated to continue pushing forward.

In addition to providing support and setting goals, it is important to cultivate a growth mindset in individuals. A growth mindset is the belief that abilities and intelligence can be developed through hard work, dedication, and perseverance. By fostering this mindset, individuals are more likely to view challenges as opportunities for growth rather than insurmountable obstacles. They are also more inclined to seek out feedback and constructive criticism as a way to improve and enhance their skills.

One way to promote a growth mindset is to emphasize the importance of effort and hard work in achieving success. By highlighting the value of persistence and dedication, individuals are more likely to stay committed to their goals and push through difficult times. It is also important to debunk the myth of innate talent or intelligence, as this can often lead individuals to believe that success is out of their control. By emphasizing the role of effort and practice in achieving success, individuals are more likely to stay motivated and focused on their goals.

Additionally, it is important to cultivate a culture of learning and continuous improvement. Encouraging individuals to seek out new challenges, explore different perspectives, and expand their knowledge can help foster a sense of curiosity and a desire for growth. By embracing a mindset of lifelong learning, individuals are more likely to stay motivated and engaged in their pursuits. It is also important to create a supportive environment where individuals feel safe to take risks, make mistakes, and learn from their experiences. By providing support, setting goals, fostering a growth mindset, and promoting a culture of learning, individuals can cultivate the resilience and determination needed to overcome challenges and reach their full potential. Encouraging individuals to believe in themselves and their ability to succeed can have a lasting impact on their academic performance, career progression, and overall well-being. By instilling these qualities in individuals, we can empower them to face the future with confidence and optimism.

Chapter 16: Navigating Parenting Challenges

- Dealing with sibling rivalry, defiance, and other common parenting struggles

Parenting can be an incredibly rewarding experience, but it also comes with its fair share of challenges. One of the most common issues that parents face is sibling rivalry. Sibling rivalry occurs when children compete for their parents' attention, affection, and resources. This can manifest in a variety of ways, such as arguing, fighting, or trying to outdo one another. While sibling rivalry is a normal part of growing up, it can be stressful for parents to manage. Fortunately, there are several strategies that parents can use to help their children navigate sibling rivalry in a healthy way.

One of the most important things that parents can do to address sibling rivalry is to set clear expectations and boundaries for their children. This can help children understand what is expected of them and reduce the likelihood of conflict. For example, parents can establish rules around sharing toys, taking turns, and resolving conflicts peacefully. By setting clear expectations, parents can help their children develop positive communication skills and learn to cooperate with one another.

In addition to setting clear expectations, parents can also encourage positive sibling relationships by fostering a sense of teamwork and cooperation. Parents can help their children see each other as allies rather than rivals by emphasizing the importance of working together to achieve common goals. This can help children develop a sense of camaraderie and mutual respect, which can reduce the likelihood of conflict and increase the likelihood of positive interactions.

Another common parenting struggle that parents often face is dealing with defiance. Defiance occurs when children refuse to comply with their parents' wishes or follow instructions. This can be frustrating for parents and lead to power struggles and conflicts. While defiance is a normal part of children's development, it can be challenging for parents to manage effectively.

One strategy that parents can use to address defiance is to offer choices and empower their children to make decisions. By giving children a sense of autonomy and control, parents can help reduce the likelihood of power struggles and encourage children to cooperate. For example, instead of issuing commands, parents can offer their children choices and allow them to choose how they want to approach a task or activity. This can help children feel more empowered and less resistant to following instructions.

In addition to offering choices, parents can also use positive reinforcement to encourage cooperation and compliance. Positive reinforcement involves rewarding children for behaving in desirable ways. This can include verbal praise, stickers, tokens, or other rewards that children find motivating. By using positive reinforcement, parents can help their children learn to associate desirable behaviors with positive outcomes and increase the likelihood of them repeating those behaviors in the future.

It is also important for parents to model respectful and effective communication with their children. Children learn how to communicate by observing their parents' interactions with them and with others. By modeling respectful and effective communication, parents can help their children develop positive communication skills and learn to express their thoughts, feelings, and needs in a healthy way.

One common parenting struggle that can arise is managing children's emotions. Children experience a wide range of emotions, from joy and excitement to anger and frustration. It is important for parents to help their children navigate these emotions in a healthy way. This can involve teaching children coping strategies, such as deep breathing, counting to ten, or taking a break when they feel overwhelmed. By helping children develop coping strategies, parents can empower them to manage their emotions effectively and reduce the likelihood of meltdowns or tantrums.

In addition to teaching coping strategies, parents can also help children develop emotional intelligence by acknowledging and validating their feelings. It is important for parents to create a safe and supportive environment where children feel comfortable expressing their emotions. By acknowledging and validating children's feelings, parents can help children feel heard and understood, which can strengthen the parent-child relationship and foster emotional resilience. By setting clear expectations, fostering positive sibling relationships, offering choices, using positive reinforcement, modeling effective communication, teaching coping strategies, and validating children's emotions, parents can navigate common parenting struggles in a healthy and supportive way. Through patience, consistency, and love, parents can help their children thrive and develop into happy, healthy, and resilient individuals.

- Seeking support and resources for overcoming parenting challenges

Parenting can be a challenging and rewarding journey, filled with ups and downs, joys and struggles. As parents, we often find ourselves facing various challenges that can test our patience, resilience, and skills. Whether it is dealing with sleepless nights, tantrums, or balancing work and family life, navigating the complexities of parenting can sometimes feel overwhelming. It is important to remember that it is okay to ask for help and seek support when facing these challenges.

One of the first steps in overcoming parenting challenges is recognizing that it is okay to not have all the answers and that no parent is perfect. Seeking support and resources can be a valuable way to gain new strategies, insights, and perspectives on how to navigate the difficulties of parenting. It is important to remember that there is no one-size-fits-all solution to parenting challenges, and what works for one family may not necessarily work for another. By reaching out for support, parents can gain a better understanding of their unique situation and find ways to overcome obstacles in a positive and effective manner.

There are a variety of resources available to parents who are seeking support in overcoming parenting challenges. Parenting classes, workshops, and support groups can provide valuable information, guidance, and resources to help parents navigate the complexities of raising children. These resources often cover a wide range of topics, including effective communication, discipline strategies, child development, and self-care. Additionally, parenting coaches and counselors can offer personalized support and guidance to help parents address specific challenges and develop effective coping strategies.

In addition to seeking out professional support, parents can also turn to friends, family members, and other parents for advice, encouragement, and solidarity. Building a support network of like-minded individuals can provide parents with a sense of community and connection, which can be invaluable during times of struggle and stress. Peer support can also offer a unique perspective and insight into different parenting styles, approaches, and experiences, which can help parents gain new insights and ideas for overcoming challenges.

Self-care is another important aspect of overcoming parenting challenges. Taking care of oneself is crucial for maintaining a healthy balance and perspective in the midst of the chaos and demands of parenting. Parents must prioritize their physical, mental, and emotional well-being to ensure that they have the energy and resilience to face challenges head-on. This may involve setting aside time for relaxation and self-reflection, engaging in activities that bring joy and fulfillment, and seeking professional support when needed.

It is important for parents to remember that they are not alone in facing parenting challenges. Seeking support and resources can provide parents with the tools, strategies, and reassurance they need to navigate the complexities of raising children. By acknowledging that it is okay to ask for help and reaching out to others for support, parents can enhance their confidence, resilience, and effectiveness in addressing parenting challenges. Remember, no parent is perfect, and it is okay to seek support and resources to help overcome obstacles and thrive in the journey of raising children.

Chapter 17: Balancing Work and Family Life

- Finding a harmonious balance between work responsibilities and family time

Finding a harmonious balance between work responsibilities and family time is a challenge that many professionals face in today's fast-paced world. With the demands of work constantly increasing and the pressure to excel in one's career becoming more intense, it can be difficult to carve out quality time for family and personal pursuits. However, striking a balance between work and family is essential for maintaining overall well-being and satisfaction in life.

One of the key factors in finding a harmonious balance between work responsibilities and family time is effective time management. By prioritizing tasks and setting boundaries between work and personal life, individuals can ensure that they are able to devote adequate time and energy to both spheres. This may involve creating a schedule or routine that allows for dedicated family time, as well as establishing clear expectations with employers about work hours and availability.

Communication is another crucial component of maintaining a balance between work and family. By openly discussing expectations and needs with both employers and family members, individuals can help to prevent misunderstandings and conflicts that can arise from competing demands. It is important to be honest about personal limitations and to ask for support when needed, whether that means delegating tasks at work or seeking help with childcare and household responsibilities.

Setting boundaries is also vital in achieving a balance between work and family. This may involve establishing clear expectations with colleagues about availability outside of work hours, as well as creating physical boundaries between work and home life, such as designating a specific room or area of the house for work-related tasks. By setting boundaries, individuals can create a sense of separation between their professional and personal lives, allowing for greater focus and engagement in each sphere.

Self-care is an essential aspect of maintaining a balance between work responsibilities and family time. It is important for individuals to prioritize their physical and emotional well-being in order to be able to effectively juggle the demands of work and family. This may involve making time for activities that bring joy and relaxation, such as exercise, hobbies, or spending time with friends. By taking care of oneself, individuals can ensure that they have the energy and resilience needed to navigate the challenges of balancing competing demands.

Flexibility is another key to finding a harmonious balance between work responsibilities and family time. In today's interconnected and fast-paced world, unexpected events and emergencies can arise that require individuals to adjust their plans and priorities. By remaining flexible and adaptable, individuals can better navigate these challenges and find creative solutions to balance their work and family responsibilities. This may involve seeking alternative work arrangements, such as telecommuting or flexible hours, in order to accommodate family commitments.

Ultimately, finding a harmonious balance between work responsibilities and family time requires a proactive and intentional approach. By prioritizing effective time management, communication, boundaries, self-care, and flexibility, individuals can create a sense of equilibrium in their lives that allows for meaningful engagement in both their professional and personal spheres. By taking the time to reflect on their priorities and values, individuals can make conscious choices that help them to achieve a sense of fulfillment and satisfaction in all aspects of their lives.

- Incorporating self-care and relaxation into your daily routine

In today's fast-paced and stressful world, taking care of yourself is more important than ever. Incorporating self-care and relaxation into your daily routine can have a significant impact on your overall well-being and quality of life. While it may seem like a luxury or indulgence, self-care is actually an essential practice that can help you manage stress, improve your mental and physical health, and enhance your productivity and creativity.

Self-care is defined as any deliberate action taken by an individual to promote their own physical, mental, and emotional well-being. This can include activities such as exercise, meditation, journaling, spending time in nature, taking a hot bath, or engaging in a hobby that brings you joy. Self-care looks different for everyone, so it's important to find activities that resonate with you and make you feel rejuvenated and refreshed.

Incorporating self-care into your daily routine doesn't have to be time-consuming or expensive. Even just a few minutes a day can make a big difference in how you feel. Prioritizing self-care can help you manage stress, reduce anxiety, and improve your overall mood. It can also help you become more resilient in the face of challenges and setbacks.

Relaxation is also a crucial component of self-care. The ability to relax and unwind is essential for maintaining a healthy work-life balance and preventing burnout. Incorporating relaxation techniques into your daily routine can help you feel more calm, centered, and present. This can improve your focus and concentration, as well as your ability to make sound decisions and solve problems effectively.

There are many different ways to incorporate self-care and relaxation into your daily routine. One approach is to schedule regular "me time" each day, where you engage in activities that bring you joy and relaxation. This could be as simple as taking a walk in nature, listening to music, or practicing yoga or meditation. Setting aside time for self-care can help you recharge your batteries and restore your energy levels.

Another approach is to practice mindfulness throughout the day. Mindfulness involves paying attention to the present moment without judgment. This can help you become more aware of your thoughts, feelings, and sensations, and cultivate a sense of inner peace and calm. You can practice mindfulness by taking a few moments to focus on your breathing, observe your surroundings, or engage in a mindful activity such as eating or walking.

Incorporating self-care and relaxation into your daily routine may require some effort and commitment, but the benefits are well worth it. By taking the time to prioritize your own well-being, you can improve your overall quality of life and enhance your resilience to stress and adversity. Remember that self-care is not selfish or indulgent – it is a necessary practice that can help you thrive and flourish in all areas of your life. So make self-care a priority in your daily routine, and watch as you become happier, healthier, and more balanced.

Chapter 18: Cultivating Gratitude and Mindfulness in Your Child

- Instilling a sense of gratitude and appreciation in your child

Instilling a sense of gratitude and appreciation in a child is a crucial aspect of their overall development. Research has shown that children who are taught to be grateful tend to be happier, more optimistic, and have stronger social relationships. By fostering a sense of gratitude in your child, you are not only helping them develop important character traits, but also setting them up for success in the future. It is essential for parents to be intentional in their efforts to instill gratitude in their children from a young age, as this will lay the foundation for their emotional well-being and resilience later in life.

One way to cultivate gratitude in your child is by modeling gratitude yourself. Children learn best by observing the behavior of their parents and caregivers, so it is important to demonstrate gratitude in your own life. This can be as simple as saying "thank you" when someone does something nice for you, or expressing appreciation for the things you have in your life. By modeling gratitude on a regular basis, you are showing your child the importance of being thankful and appreciative of the people and things around them.

Another effective way to instill gratitude in your child is by encouraging them to practice gratitude on a daily basis. This can be done through activities such as keeping a gratitude journal, where your child can write down things they are thankful for each day. By having your child reflect on the positive things in their life, they will develop a greater appreciation for the things they have and the people who support them. Encouraging your child to express gratitude verbally, such as saying thank you to others or acknowledging acts of kindness, will also help reinforce this important value.

It is important for parents to create a culture of gratitude in their homes, where expressions of appreciation are common and encouraged. This can be done by creating rituals or traditions that promote gratitude, such as having a family gratitude circle before dinner where everyone shares something they are thankful for. By making gratitude a part of your family's routine, you are reinforcing the importance of being thankful and appreciative in your child's mind. This will help them develop a positive outlook on life and foster healthy relationships with others.

Teaching your child to be grateful also involves helping them understand the concept of perspective. Children may not always realize the privileges and blessings they have compared to others, so it is important for parents to expose them to different perspectives and experiences. This can be done through volunteering as a family, where your child can see firsthand the challenges that others may face and learn to appreciate the things they may take for granted. By broadening your child's perspective, you are helping them develop empathy and a deeper understanding of the world around them. By modeling gratitude, encouraging daily practices of gratitude, creating a culture of appreciation in your home, and teaching your child about perspective, you are helping them develop important character traits that will benefit them throughout their lives. By nurturing gratitude in your child, you are setting them up for success and happiness in the future.

- Practicing mindfulness and being present in the moment with your child

In today's fast-paced world, it can be easy to get caught up in our hectic schedules and endless to-do lists. However, it is essential to take the time to practice mindfulness and be present in the moment with our children. Mindfulness is the practice of being fully present and engaged in the current moment, without judgment or distraction. By practicing mindfulness with our children, we can strengthen our relationships, improve communication, and create a sense of peace and calm in our homes.

Being present with our children means giving them our full attention and focusing on the here and now. It means putting aside our worries about the past or future and truly connecting with our child in the present moment. This can be as simple as sitting down and playing with them, listening to their stories, or engaging in a mindful activity together like coloring or going for a walk. By being fully present with our children, we show them that we value and care about them, which can help strengthen our bond and create a sense of security and stability in their lives.

Practicing mindfulness with our children can also improve our communication with them. When we are fully present and focused on our child, we are better able to listen to what they are saying, understand their feelings and needs, and respond in a thoughtful and caring way. This can help foster open and honest communication between us and our children, which is essential for building trust and a strong parent-child relationship. By practicing mindfulness and being present in the moment with our children, we can create a safe and supportive environment where they feel heard, understood, and validated.

In addition to improving our relationships and communication with our children, practicing mindfulness can also help us as parents to reduce stress and manage our emotions more effectively. When we are present in the moment, we are better able to notice our thoughts and feelings as they arise, without getting caught up in them or reacting impulsively. This can help us to stay calm and focused, even in challenging situations, and respond to our children in a caring and compassionate way. By practicing mindfulness regularly, we can cultivate a sense of inner peace and balance that can benefit both us and our children.

There are many simple and practical ways to practice mindfulness with our children on a daily basis. One effective strategy is to set aside dedicated time each day to engage in a mindful activity together, such as reading a book, doing a puzzle, or taking a walk. During this time, focus on being fully present with your child, paying attention to their words, actions, and emotions without judgment or distraction. You can also practice mindfulness in everyday activities, such as eating a meal together or doing chores around the house. Encourage your child to pay attention to their senses and savor the experience of being in the moment with you.

It is important to remember that practicing mindfulness with our children is a journey, not a destination. It takes time and effort to cultivate a mindful presence and create a deeper connection with our children. Be patient with yourself and your child as you work on this practice together, and remember that every moment of mindfulness counts. By being present in the moment with your child, you can create a sense of peace, joy, and connection that will benefit both of you for years to come.

Chapter 19: Strengthening Your Parenting Skills for Long-Term Success

- Continuing to learn and grow as a parent

As parents, our journey is a continuous process of learning and growth. From the moment our children are born, we are faced with new challenges and opportunities that shape our understanding of what it means to be a parent. It is important to recognize that we do not have all the answers and that there is always room for improvement. By embracing a mindset of continued learning and growth, we can better support our children's development and create a more positive and fulfilling parenting experience.

One of the key aspects of continuing to learn and grow as a parent is staying open to new ideas and perspectives. Parenting is not a one-size-fits-all approach, and what works for one family may not work for another. By being open to different viewpoints and approaches, we can expand our understanding of parenting and discover new strategies that may be more effective for our unique circumstances. This willingness to learn from others can help us adapt our parenting style to better meet the needs of our children and create a more harmonious family dynamic.

Another important aspect of continuing to learn and grow as a parent is self-reflection. It is essential to regularly evaluate our parenting practices and consider how our actions and behaviors may be impacting our children. By taking the time to reflect on our strengths and weaknesses as parents, we can identify areas where we can improve and make positive changes for the benefit of our children. Self-reflection allows us to become more self-aware and better equipped to address any challenges that may arise in our parenting journey.

In addition to staying open to new ideas and engaging in self-reflection, seeking out resources and support can also be valuable in continuing to learn and grow as a parent. There are a wealth of resources available to parents, including books, online articles, parenting workshops, and support groups, that can provide valuable insights and guidance on various aspects of parenting. By actively seeking out information and support from these sources, we can expand our knowledge and skills as parents and gain new perspectives on how to navigate the complexities of raising children.

Furthermore, continuing to learn and grow as a parent also involves prioritizing self-care. Parenting can be a demanding and exhausting role, and it is important to take care of ourselves so that we can be better equipped to care for our children. This means making time for activities that bring us joy and relaxation, prioritizing our physical and mental health, and seeking out support from friends, family, or professionals when needed. By prioritizing self-care, we can cultivate a sense of well-being that allows us to be more present and attentive parents for our children. By embracing this mindset of continual learning and growth, we can better support our children's development, strengthen our family relationships, and create a more positive and fulfilling parenting experience. Ultimately, our willingness to adapt and grow as parents will not only benefit our children but also contribute to our own personal growth and well-being.

- Reflecting on your parenting journey and setting goals for improvement

Parenting is a lifelong journey filled with ups and downs, challenges and triumphs. As parents, we strive to provide the best possible upbringing for our children, but it is inevitable that mistakes will be made along the way. It is important to take the time to reflect on our parenting journey, to acknowledge our successes and shortcomings, and to set goals for improvement.

Reflecting on our parenting journey can be a powerful tool for growth and self-improvement. By taking the time to examine our parenting practices, we can gain valuable insights into what is working well and what areas may need improvement. It is important to approach this reflection with an open mind and a willingness to be honest with ourselves. This can be a challenging process, as it may require us to confront aspects of our parenting that we are not proud of.

However, by facing these challenges head-on, we can take steps to make positive changes for the benefit of our children.

One aspect of reflecting on our parenting journey is examining the values and beliefs that shape our approach to parenting. Our own upbringing, cultural background, and personal experiences all play a role in shaping the way we parent our children. It is important to consider how these influences impact our parenting style and to reflect on whether they align with the values and goals we have for our family. For example, if we were raised in a strict, authoritarian household, we may find ourselves defaulting to a similar parenting style, even if it does not align with our desire to foster independence and autonomy in our children. By reflecting on these influences, we can make conscious choices about the kind of parent we want to be and the values we want to instill in our children.

Another important aspect of reflecting on our parenting journey is examining our strengths and weaknesses as parents. We all have areas where we excel and areas where we struggle, and it is important to be honest about these strengths and weaknesses. For example, some parents may excel at setting boundaries and providing structure, while struggling with emotional expression and connection. Others may excel at nurturing and empathy, while struggling with consistency and follow-through. By acknowledging our strengths and weaknesses, we can make informed decisions about where we need to focus our efforts for improvement.

Setting goals for improvement is a key step in the process of reflecting on our parenting journey. Once we have identified areas for growth and development, it is important to set specific, measurable, achievable, relevant, and time-bound (SMART) goals to guide our efforts. For example, if we identify that we struggle with maintaining consistency in our discipline practices, a SMART goal might be to establish a daily routine for addressing behavior issues and to track our progress over the course of a month. By setting clear goals and monitoring our progress, we can hold ourselves accountable for making positive changes in our parenting practices.

It is also important to seek support and guidance as we work towards our parenting goals. Parenting can be a challenging and isolating experience, and it is important to reach out to others for support. This may include seeking advice from friends, family members, or professionals, participating in parenting workshops or support groups, or seeking counseling or therapy. By surrounding ourselves with a supportive network of individuals who share our values and goals, we can gain valuable insights, perspective, and encouragement to help us navigate the complexities of parenting. By taking the time to examine our values and beliefs, strengths and weaknesses, and areas for growth, we can make informed decisions about the kind of parent we want to be and the values we want to instill in our children. By setting clear, achievable goals and seeking support and guidance, we can make positive changes in our parenting practices and create a nurturing and supportive environment for our children to thrive. Parenting is a journey that requires continuous learning and growth, and by engaging in this process of reflection and goal-setting, we can become the best possible parents for our children.

Chapter 20: Conclusion

- Summary of key takeaways from the book

One of the key takeaways from the book is the importance of understanding the historical context in which the topic is situated. By examining key events and developments that have shaped the field, readers can gain a deeper understanding of the subject matter and its implications for the present day.

Another key takeaway from the book is the emphasis on interdisciplinary approaches to the topic. The author highlights how insights from diverse fields such as sociology, psychology, and economics can help shed light on different aspects of the topic and provide a more nuanced understanding of its complexities. This interdisciplinary approach also allows for a more holistic perspective that takes into account the multiple factors that influence the topic.

Additionally, the book emphasizes the need for critical thinking and analytical skills when engaging with the topic. By questioning assumptions, challenging prevailing ideas, and examining evidence from multiple perspectives, readers can develop a more nuanced understanding of the topic and avoid falling into simplistic or reductive interpretations. The author provides valuable guidance on how to cultivate these skills and apply them to the study of the topic.

One of the key insights from the book is the recognition of the diversity of perspectives and voices within the field. By engaging with a range of perspectives, readers can develop a more comprehensive and nuanced understanding of the topic and its implications for various stakeholders.

The book also underscores the importance of ethical considerations when engaging with the topic. The author discusses key ethical principles and guidelines that should guide research and practice in the field, including respect for autonomy, beneficence, and justice. By applying these ethical principles to their own work, readers can ensure that their efforts are conducted in a responsible and respectful manner that upholds the well-being and dignity of all individuals involved. By examining key concepts, engaging with diverse perspectives, and applying critical thinking skills, readers can develop a more nuanced and informed perspective on the topic. The book serves as a valuable guide for students, scholars, and practitioners alike, offering insights and tools to navigate the complexities of the field with confidence and clarity.

- Encouragement for parents to continue applying successful parenting strategies for raising happy and responsible kids.

Raising children is undoubtedly one of the most important and rewarding tasks a parent can undertake. However, it is also one of the most challenging. As parents, we all want our children to grow up to be happy, responsible, and well-adjusted individuals. This requires a great deal of time, effort, and dedication on our part. It is essential to remember that raising children is a long-term commitment and that the strategies we employ today will have a lasting impact on our children's development and future success.

One of the key elements in raising happy and responsible children is consistency. Consistency in our parenting approach helps to provide a sense of security and predictability for our children. When we are consistent in our rules, expectations, and consequences, our children learn what is expected of them and how to meet those expectations. Consistency also helps to establish a routine and structure in our children's lives, which can help them feel safe and secure. By being consistent in our parenting, we can help our children develop self-discipline, responsibility, and good decision-making skills.

Another important aspect of successful parenting is communication. By fostering open and honest communication with our children, we can strengthen our bond with them and help them feel valued and respected. It is essential to listen to our children's thoughts, feelings, and concerns, and to provide them with guidance, support, and encouragement. Communication is a two-way street, and it is important to not only talk to our children but also to listen to what they have to say. By establishing a positive and supportive communication style, we can create a nurturing and loving environment for our children to thrive in.

In addition to consistency and communication, positive reinforcement is also a crucial element in successful parenting. Positive reinforcement involves acknowledging and rewarding our children's good behavior, effort, and accomplishments. By offering praise, encouragement, and rewards for positive behavior, we can help our children build self-esteem, confidence, and a sense of achievement. Positive reinforcement can also help to motivate our children to continue their efforts and strive for success. It is important to be specific in our praise and to focus on our children's efforts and progress rather than just their achievements. By using positive reinforcement effectively, we can create a supportive and encouraging environment that empowers our children to reach their full potential.

Another essential aspect of successful parenting is setting boundaries and providing structure for our children. Boundaries help to establish rules of conduct and limits for our children, which can help them develop self-control, self-discipline, and respect for others. By setting clear and consistent boundaries, we can help our children understand the difference between right and wrong, and help them learn how to make good choices and decisions. It is important to be firm but fair when setting boundaries and to enforce them consistently. By providing structure and boundaries for our children, we can help them feel secure, safe, and supported, which can help them grow into responsible and well-adjusted individuals.

To summarize, it is essential to remember that parenting is a journey, not a destination. As parents, we will make mistakes, face challenges, and encounter obstacles along the way. It is important to be patient, forgiving, and flexible with ourselves and with our children. Parenting is a learning process, and we will continue to grow and evolve as parents as our children grow and develop. It is important to seek support and guidance from other parents, educators, and professionals when needed, and to be open to new ideas, perspectives, and approaches to parenting. By staying committed, dedicated, and resilient in our parenting efforts, we can continue to apply successful strategies for raising happy and responsible children who will thrive and succeed in life.